OREGON

A PICTURE MEMORY

CLB 2515
© 1990 Colour Library Books Ltd., Godalming, Surrey, England.
All rights reserved.
This 1990 edition is published by Crescent Books,
distributed by Outlet Book Company, Inc., a Random House Company,
40 Engelhard Avenue, Avenel, New Jersey 07001.

Random House
New York • Toronto • London • Sydney • Auckland

Printed and bound in Singapore

ISBN 0-517-02541-8

9 8 7 6 5 4

Text
Bill Harris

Captions
Pauline Graham

Design
Teddy Hartshorn

Photography
Black Star
Colour Library Books Ltd
FPG International
International Stock Photo

Picture Editor
Annette Lerner

Commissioning Editor
Andrew Preston

Publishing Assistant
Edward Doling

Editorial
Gill Waugh
Pauline Graham

Production
Ruth Arthur
Sally Connolly
David Proffit
Andrew Whitelaw

Director of Production
Gerald Hughes

Director of Publishing
David Gibbon

OREGON
A PICTURE MEMORY

CRESCENT BOOKS
NEW YORK / AVENEL, NEW JERSEY

Enhydra lutris started it all. It drove men mad with greed. It caused a stir in the highest levels of government in four countries. It caused many explorers to abandon their quest for the Northwest Passage that had been their "Holy Grail" for more than three centuries. It inspired thousands to rank the name Oregon as highly in their imaginations as El Dorado.

Yet the Enhydra is scarcely such a significant-looking beast. It is a four-foot-long, web-footed creature known in some cultures as the sea beaver, but is familiar to most of us as the sea otter. Its dark brown fur looks almost black in the waters of the northern Pacific, but when it is stroked it has a silver sheen. Its waterproof underfur is unusually thick, and as soft as silk. Indeed, if God had fur coats for humans in mind when He created fur-bearing animals, the sea otter was to be without question the most prized of them.

Russian explorers who sailed to the North American coast from Siberia during the second quarter of the eighteenth century found little to impress them on their eight-year voyage, but they impressed their countrymen by clearing a profit of nearly 10,000 gold rubles by selling sea-otter pelts hunted in North America to Chinese merchants. Within a year or two the men who followed them were counting their profits in millions.

Hearing news of this invasion of Russian hunters, the Spanish, who had been granted all of North America by a papal bull just after Columbus arrived on the other side of the continent, dispatched ships to check it out and to strengthen their claim to its northwest corner. Moreover, the English, who were having trouble with a rebellion in their colonies on the East Coast, decided it was time to become serious about the search for a waterway across the top of North America.

That assignment fell to Captain James Cook who, coincidentally, discovered the Hawaiian Islands on his voyage. Cook did not find the Northwest Passage, but his men traded with the Indians for coats made of sea otter skins, which they thought would provide perfect protection against the bitter cold they would have to face when they pushed further north. Instead, however, Cook had to turn back to Hawaii, where he met an untimely end. His ships eventually made their way to Canton, where the Chinese could hardly believe their eyes when they noticed that some of the sailors were wearing sea otter coats. Up until then the English had had no idea of the value of sea otter skins, and some had

even been using the prized fur as lining for their sea chests. The Russians had guarded their commercial secret very well. Even the normally suspicious Spanish had not bothered to question why the Russians were so willing to endure the hardships of life on the Northwest Coast. When the Chinese offered them hundreds of pounds for coats they had bought for a few brass buttons, the British sailors could scarcely believe their luck. Suddenly voyages to the frozen North seemed like a dream assignment, even without a Northwest Passage to make the trip shorter.

By then, the English colonies in America had established themselves as an independent country, and a group of Boston merchants had read reports of the Cook expedition. Trade with the Orient was their goal, and sea otter skins represented the best possible medium of exchange. In the summer of 1788, a pair of American ships, *Columbia Rediviva* and the *Lady Washington*, loaded with trinkets to trade for furs, sailed up the Oregon Coast. The Indians were not impressed. English ships had been coming and going for four years by then, and the natives liked their trinkets more than the things the Americans had to offer. But Yankee ingenuity saved the day. They found that the Indians liked chisels the Americans had fashioned from bits of iron and that, possibly bored by brass buttons and cooking utensils, they were more than willing to swap them for furs.

The Spanish were in the area too, showing the flag and threatening English and Russian adventurers. However, though they seized foreign ships and took their crews prisoner, they were friendly to the American captains Robert Gray and John Kendrick. It allowed the New Englanders to remain beyond the battle and collect their pelts relatively unmolested. His hold filled, Gray took the *Columbia* on to China and then sailed back to Boston. As it turned out, Gray was a better sailor than trader. His trip did not produce the hoped-for profits, but it made *Columbia* the first American ship to sail around the world, and the consequent prestige was worth more than money to a country with dreams of becoming a world power.

As the Spanish and the English were rattling their sabres at each other over their territorial rights in the Pacific Northwest, Robert Gray set sail aboard *Columbia* again, this time with nearly 5,000 little chisels in her hold. The international tensions he encountered when he arrived back at Nootka Sound, on present-day

Vancouver Island, prompted him to turn his attention southward to where earlier explorers and friendly Indians had described a great river, which they called the Oregon. A generation earlier, it had been a contender for the Pacific end of what was hoped to be the Northwest Passage, but Gray was not thinking of that. What he wanted was a suitable harbor at which to set up a trading post away from direct competition. On May 11, 1792, he found the river and renamed it Columbia for his ship.

The English explorer George Vancouver followed Gray's directions to the mouth of the Columbia, but he never managed to cross the breakers to explore it and soon went home having arrived at the conclusion that there was no such thing as a Northwest Passage. Gray did not bother to explore the river either because it was apparent that there were no sea otters in it. However, in the time-honored tradition of exploration, he claimed the Columbia region as the property of his native country, the United States.

It is hard to imagine that less than 200 years ago no white man had bothered to explore this fabulous countryside. Neither had any seen Crater Lake, nor climbed the Cascade Mountains. Not one had smelled the flowers in the Willamette River Valley or even dreamed that there were deserts a few hundred miles away from the most lush pine forests on the continent. What is easy to imagine, on the other hand, is that the British had no intention of letting the Northwest slip though their fingers, even if Robert Gray's claim to the Columbia was every bit as valid as their claim to North America based on the voyages of Sir Francis Drake.

In a way, the sea otter was also at the bottom of the eventual rush to explore this land. In the years after Cook's sailors discovered the creature's value, Europeans very nearly hunted it to extinction, which resulted in fortune hunters having to look inland for money-making opportunities. During those years, England had managed to negotiate a treaty with the Spanish for control of the area, and they had taken possession of all of Canada from the French. The big question was whether the Oregon Territory was part of Canada or part of the United States, and the question was commercially very important when the incredible number of beaver skins that could be taken from it was considered.

The French had exploited the beaver trade into the

Rocky Mountains, but were frustrated by the problem of shipping supplies from the East Coast and getting their pelts back out to market. The Hudson Bay Company partly solved that problem for themselves through exclusive use of Hudson Bay, which extends inland halfway across Canada as far west as Manitoba. With the French out of the way, opportunists from the United States and Canada filled the vacuum by setting up the North West Fur Company in competition with the Bay Company. However, both competitors still had a transportation problem.

In 1793, Alexander Mackenzie trekked across Canada, proving it could be done, but his effort did not impress either the competing fur companies or the British Government, which he warned to develop a transcontinental land route before American adventurers beat them to it. In fact, the adventurer who took Mackenzie's warning most seriously was the new American President, Thomas Jefferson. He had just negotiated with Napoleon for control of territory west of the Mississippi, which technically ended at the Rocky Mountains, but he was also intrigued by the river which Gray had found in Oregon. He wondered if it might reach to the Missouri River, providing America with an answer to the problem of overland travel from sea to sea. On the pretext of advancing scientific knowledge, he sent an expedition headed by his former secretary, Meriwether Lewis, and Army officer, William Clark, to make the trip from St. Louis to the mouth of the Columbia River.

It took Alexander Mackenzie four years to hike across the continent. Lewis and Clark made it in nineteen months. Neither expedition had an easy time of it, but like all of mankind's accomplishments, the fact that they succeeded at all encouraged others to follow. After establishing a camp at Fort Clatsop on the Oregon coast and wintering there, Lewis and Clark began their long trip back, taking time to explore territory they had missed on their westward trip. At the same time, Canadian explorers were mapping the territory north of the 49th parallel, following Mackenzie's advice to make it their own before the Americans could move in on them.

Five more years passed before the Americans made their next move. In 1811, John Jacob Astor, who had already made an enviable fortune in the fur trade, decided to follow the route of Lewis and Clark to establish a monopoly trade on the West Coast First he negotiated with the Russians, who were still trapping in

Alaska and had ranged as far down the coast as California, to supply their trappers and transport their furs to China for sale. His proposition indirectly defused a threat of further Russian establishment in the Pacific Northwest, as would perhaps have been inevitable if Russian supply people had had to move in to service their hunters. However, no amount of scheming could secure him a similar agreement with the Canadians. Undaunted, he went into competition with them and sent men to build an outpost in Oregon and establish his Pacific Fur Company there. It was an American enterprise, but Astor covered his bets by hiring the best and brightest trappers and executives from the North West Company. He dispatched them to the Northwest aboard one of his own ships from New York and, as additional insurance, he sent a second party overland. The ship arrived first and established the first American settlement in Oregon, naming it Astoria in honor of their mentor. By the time the overland party arrived, the United States and Britain were rushing headlong into a war with each other and the Astor contingent began to receive reports that a British warship was on its way to capture them. They forestalled any confrontation by selling the fort to the Canadians, and America lost its foothold in Oregon. Mr. Astor lost $120,000, and his immortality in the Northwest was threatened when the English renamed his post Fort George.

The treaty that ended the war returned the territory to the United States, but Astor decided he did not want to trade there anymore and the Hudson Bay Company filled the vacuum he left by setting up its own headquarters of the banks of the Columbia. Their scheme was to keep the Yankees out of Oregon and eventually make the river the boundary between the United States and Canada. They very nearly succeeded.

Though trading in beaver skins was their principle business, beaver hats had suddenly gone out of style and the market was drying up. The Bay Company responded by expanding into lumbering and farming, and they not only turned good profits, but established industries that have not stopped producing yet. By the 1830s, Oregon, though on paper it belonged to the United States, was as much a British colony as Boston had ever been.

However, in 1831, back in Boston, Hall Jackson Kelley had a visit from God. He claimed that this visitation was to prompt him to form the American Society for Encouraging Settlement of the Oregon Country. He began distributing handbills and posters all over New England in order to raise a company of 5,000 to settle a place that he had never seen, but that God had apparently assured him was the new Eden. He was not able to persuade more than a few dozen to "Go West," but he went himself, eventually coming back to New England where he began his campaign all over again – this time armed with first-hand information. Among the people he impressed this time was Nathaniel Jarvis Wyeth, a less wild-eyed zealot than himself, who sold stock in what he called the Columbia River Fishing & Trading Company, and he set out for the West to give the Bay Company a little competition.

The Bay Company traders welcomed him into their midst, but he was no match for them – many said because he was too honest – and he eventually returned to New England as Kelley had done. However, among the people who went overland with him, a pair of Methodist Missionaries, Jason Lee and his nephew Daniel, stayed behind in the Willamette Valley where they began organizing the other settlers to petition the United States for a Territorial Government. Their petition fell on deaf ears back in Washington, but Jason Lee was a determined man. He marched overland to present the petition in person. Moreover, during the year he was back in the East he encouraged more settlers to follow him to Oregon. He also succeeded in convincing Congress to give its blessing to an expansion of American influence into the Northwest.

The Bay Company responded by importing Canadian settlers, but the die was cast. In 1843, "Oregon Fever" gripped the United States: 900 Americans arrived over the Oregon Trail. The following year twice as many made the trip and, in 1845, 3,000 more arrived, bringing the American flag with them.

To these people the goal of reaching Oregon seemed worth their hardships. En route they even passed on good farmland the government was offering for $1.25 an acre. They were prepared and eager to invest their savings, even to risk their lives, in transporting themselves and their families to Oregon instead. They had never seen Oregon, but they knew instinctively that the trees were taller there, the fish were fatter, the game was more abundant and, yes, the grass was greener. Besides, that land on the other side of the mountains was free.

It was only a matter of time before the settlers began to spill over into territory north of the Columbia, which presented the Hudson Bay Company with a problem. But if the men of the Bay were tough and hard-nosed, the Americans, hardened by their long trip across the continent, were tougher. In London, Parliament began talking about going to war to protect the Bay's interests, and in Washington even the coolest heads were saying, "Let them come!" But neither side really wanted a war, especially in such a remote spot as Oregon was in 1846. The Americans were already facing the prospect of a war with Mexico over Texas, so eventually President James Polk decided that the longed-for Northwest border set at 54° 40' might be excessive after all and agreed to compromise by setting it along the 49th parallel – the accepted border between the United States and Canada in the East. Two years later, Oregon was officially designated a Territory, and a decade after that it became the 33rd State.

Oregon Territory was called the Inland Empire. Wheat grew so fast in mile upon mile of volcanic soil that it was said a man could hardly catch his breath between planting and harvesting. Most of the soil's moisture was provided by light winter snow that protected the plants. Spring days were warm and dry, and hail – which had ruined many a wheat crop back in the Midwest – was unknown there. Furthermore, there was a wonderful cash crop already in place: the area between the Cascades and the Pacific was covered with the biggest virgin forest in all of the United States. Douglas fir and gigantic cedars covered the land, and near the sea the forests were filled with spruce and hemlock. The Hudson Bay Company had begun cutting them down, and by the 1850s a steam sawmill in Portland was exporting lumber all over the world. It was scarcely a coincidence that the city was named for another in Maine ....

When pioneers from the Pine Tree State began arriving, they could hardly believe their eyes. State O'Mainers had been cutting trees since the earliest colonial times. In fact, the British had first colonized the Northeast Coast specifically to cut masts for their ships. None of the settlers had seen anything like the Douglas fir and, for the first time, American pioneers began to look to the commercial value of trees.

The land was well worth fighting for and the Indians, who considered Oregon to be their own in spite of the Hudson Bay Company, began to fight the missionaries, farmers, loggers and salmon fishermen, not to mention the Congress of the United States, for their homeland. Their battles for eastern and central Oregon lasted for twenty years before the coming of the railroads brought so many more white men that the Indians could no longer fight them all. When the government solved the problem by moving the native Americans to reservations, the ranchers and farmers began fighting among themselves.

However, by the beginning of the twentieth century, Oregon had become a relatively peaceful place. Trading posts had become cities and frontier forts thriving towns. Rivers were dammed, railroads built and canals dug. The landscape was altered, but not changed. What has changed least of all is the fierce independence of the Oregon folk themselves.

In recent years, people who had migrated to California looking for a better life started to discover that the best lifestyle to be had was further up the coast, and began moving there. An influx of Californians has changed the general outlook in some parts of Oregon but, despite occasional disputes, the locals and the newcomers are learning to trust one another because, in the end, they have one thing in common. They all love this place called Oregon.

The Snake River (these pages and overleaf) forms a natural boundary between Oregon and Idaho, and its 125-mile-long Hells Canyon is the continent's deepest river gorge. For forty miles of its length its cliffs tower over a mile in height.

Much of Oregon's countryside has a tamed look about it now through the labors of generations of settlers. Facing page: (top) Wallowa Lake, near Joseph, and (bottom) pasture below the Wallowa Mountains. Below: golden fields near Pendleton, combed by harvest blades.

Above: sunset over scrub land west of Brothers, and (above left) bathers in Wallowa Lake. Roads now traverse much of Oregon, creating a tarmacadam trail for travellers. Below: the highway near Stanfield and (facing page bottom) the road to Kah-Nee-Ta resort in Warm Springs Indian Reservation. Left: a bridge spanning the Crooked River in Peter Skene Ogden State Park near Richmond. This river also winds through Smith Rock State Park (facing page top). Below left: La Grande, an agricultural town near Pendleton.

Facing page: Sunrise Lodge in central Oregon's Bachelor Mountain Ski Area on Mount Bachelor (right and below right). From the summit of Mount Bachelor (below) the peaks of the Three Sisters and Broken Top (above right) can be clearly seen. Above: snow-wrapped Crater Lake Lodge. Overleaf: the chocolate and white piebald peaks of the Three Sisters in spring.

Below: the North Umpqua River swirling its way through Umpqua National Forest. Right: a broken cup of mountain land in Crater Lake National Park, and (below right) Lake Abert in southern Oregon. Bottom right: a long, roller coaster-like road undulates through Umpqua National Forest near Crater Lake.

Wizard Island (facing page and below left) rises out of the 1,932-foot-deep waters of Crater Lake (left) like the back of a great, barnacle-encrusted whale. Above: the island looking like the infamous Moby Dick in winter. Below: Vidae Fall in Crater Lake National Park (these pages).

Eugene (facing page top), in the southern Willamette Valley, is one of the state's largest cities. It is home to the University of Oregon (facing page bottom), founded in 1872. Above right: Eugene's 5th Street Public Market, and (right and below right) the Eugene City Center Mall shopping area. The State University of Oregon (below) is found at Corvallis. Above: a charming 1886 Victorian house on 7th Avenue, Albany, preserved as a café and hotel. Overleaf: farm buildings east of the timber town of Roseburg.

Salem (these pages and overleaf), the historic capital of Oregon, contains many fine, old buildings. It was founded in 1840 by Methodist missionary Jason Lee, and has grown steadily since. Facing page and overleaf: the State Capitol Building, topped with its twenty-four-foot-high, gold-leafed statue The Pioneer. Above right: the bronze State Seal in the entrance hall of the Capitol, decorated with friezes depicting the history of Oregon State. Above: Bush House, built in the 1870s, and (right, below and below right) Deepwood House.

Mount Hood (facing page top) is, at 11,235 feet, the highest peak in Oregon, dominating the Cascade Range and offering year-round skiing. It is seen to great advantage from Trillium Lake (below). Facing page bottom: Warm Springs River, flowing through the Warm Springs Indian Reservation to the south of Mount Hood.

Long ago, a plague afflicted the Multnomah people, for which the only cure was the sacrifice of a maiden prepared to throw herself from the cliffs of Multnomah Falls (facing page) on the Columbia River to the rocks below. When the chief's daughter saw her love sicken, she climbed Oregon's highest falls and threw herself to her death, saving her people. Right and below: the Columbia River in Oneonta Gorge, and (below right) Sahalie Falls. Above: Wahkeena Falls, and (above right) Latourell Falls. Overleaf: South Falls in Silver Falls State Park.

Portland (these pages and overleaf), the "City of Roses,"
stands on the Willamette River, south of its junction with the
Columbia River. A claim was filed for the land in 1844 and,
later on, Francis Pettygrove and Asa Lovejoy – then the claim
owners – flipped a copper coin for the right to name it.
Pettygrove, a State O'Mainer, wanted Portland, while Lovejoy,
from Massachusetts, favored Boston. The enterprise of early
settlers and the Californian gold rush contributed to the
growth of Oregon's largest city.

Above: Washington Park in Portland, and (facing page bottom) the 1846, Georgian Revival John McLoughlin House in Oregon City. The magnificent Pittock Mansion (remaining pictures) lies in the hills west of the Willamette River. This twenty-two-room French Renaissance Revival house was built in 1914 by Henry Pittock, the owner and publisher of Portland's Daily Oregonian *paper.*

Facing page top: the beautiful International Rose Test Gardens of Portland (these pages), and (facing page bottom and right) the tranquil Japanese Gardens, both in Washington Park. Below: tramlines on Portland's 1st Avenue, and (above and below left) Pioneer Courthouse Square in the center of downtown Portland.

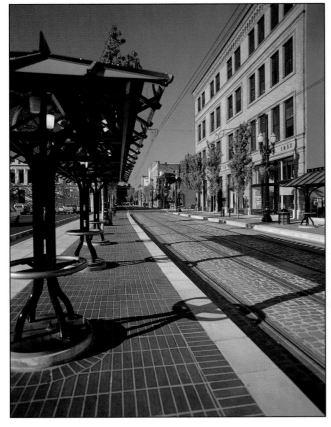

Below: a summer evening concert in Washington Park, Portland (these pages and overleaf). The solid, modern buildings of Oregon's largest city appear almost insubstantial by night when their many-colored lights blur and glitter, reflected in the Willamette River.

Facing page top: the bridge over the Columbia River, linking Astoria with Washington State. Cannon Beach (facing page bottom) stretches for seven miles between Tillamook Head and Arch Cape in northern Oregon. Above: Brookings Harbor, and (right) Yaquina Bay Bridge over Newport. Above right: Steller sea lions near the Sea Lion Caves, overlooked by Heceta Head Lighthouse (below). The 1950 lightship Columbia (below right) stood at the entrance of the Columbia River for thirty years as a marker. Overleaf: Harris Beach State Park.

Facing page: (top) the sandstone coast of Shore Acres State Park, and (bottom and final page) Harris Beach State Park. Above: a secluded beach near Pistol River, and (above right) Samuel H. Boardman State Park. Right: the view south along Heceta Beach toward Florence, and (below) the south shore of Cannon Beach. Overleaf: Haystack Rock on Cannon Beach. Below right: Netarts Bay, between Cape Meares and Cape Lookout.